SOMEWHERE IN AMERICA ...

EVERY HOUR
SOMEONE COMMITS A HATE CRIME.

EVERY DAY
AT LEAST EIGHT BLACKS, THREE WHITES, THREE GAYS, THREE JEWS AND ONE LATINO BECOME HATE CRIME VICTIMS.

EVERY WEEK
A CROSS IS BURNED.

Hate in America is a dreadful, daily constant. The dragging death of a black man in Jasper, Texas; the crucifixion of a gay man in Laramie, Wyoming; and hate crimes against hundreds of Arab-Americans are not "isolated incidents." They are eruptions of a nation's intolerance.

Bias is a human condition, and American history is rife with prejudice against groups and individuals because of their race, religion, disability, sexual orientation or other differences. The 20th Century saw major progress in outlawing discrimination, and most Americans today support integrated schools and neighborhoods. But stereotypes and unequal treatment persist, an atmosphere often exploited by hate groups.

When bias motivates an unlawful act, it is considered a hate crime. Race and religion inspire most hate crimes, but hate today wears many faces.

The greatest growth in hate crimes in recent years is against Asian-Americans and homosexuals, according to FBI statistics. Once considered a Southern phenomenon, today most hate crimes take place in the North and West. In the late 1990s there were more public Ku Klux Klan rallies, complete with white sheets, in Pennsylvania than in Alabama. In states with large immigrant populations, such as California, hate often erupts between people of color. Spread on the Internet and accessible by personal computers, hate clearly knows no geographic bounds.

THE GOOD NEWS IS ...

All over the country people are fighting hate. Standing up to hate mongers. Promoting tolerance and inclusion. More often than not, when hate flares up, good erupts, too.

This guide sets out 10 principles for fighting hate along with a collection of inspiring stories of people who acted, often alone at first, to push hate out of their communities. Their efforts usually made smaller headlines than the acts of the haters, but they made a difference. Even in the wake of some of the most horrific hate crimes of the last century, seeds of promise sprouted.

Whether you need a crash course to deal with an upcoming white power rally, a primer on the media or a long-range plan to promote tolerance in your community, you will find practical advice, good examples and additional sources in this guide. The steps outlined here have been tested in scores of communities across the U.S. by a wide range of human rights, religious and civic organizations. Our experience shows that one person, acting from conscience and love, can neutralize bigotry. A group of people can create a moral barrier to hate.

TEN WAYS TO

1 ACT

Do something. In the face of hatred, apathy will be interpreted as acceptance — by the haters, the public and, worse, the victim. Decency must be exercised, too. If it isn't, hate invariably persists.

2 UNITE

Call a friend or co-worker. Organize a group of allies from churches, schools, clubs and other civic sources. Create a diverse coalition. Include children, police and the media. Gather ideas from everyone, and get everyone involved.

3 SUPPORT THE VICTIMS

Hate-crime victims are especially vulnerable, fearful and alone. Let them know you care. Surround them with people they feel comfortable with. If you're a victim, report every incident and ask for help.

4 DO YOUR HOMEWORK

Determine if a hate group is involved, and research its symbols and agenda. Seek advice from anti-hate organizations. Accurate information can then be spread to the community.

5 CREATE AN ALTERNATIVE

Do NOT attend a hate rally. Find another outlet for anger and frustration and people's desire to do something. Hold a unity rally or parade. Find a news hook, like a "hate-free zone."

Copyright © 2000 by the Southern Poverty Law Center

Second edition, second printing

The Southern Poverty Law Center is a nonprofit legal and educational organization based in Montgomery, Alabama. The Center's co-founders are Morris S. Dees, Jr., and Joseph J. Levin, Jr. Its directors are Patricia Clark, Frances Green, Judge Rufus Huffman, Joseph J. Levin, Jr., Howard Mandell and James McElroy.

All rights reserved. No part of this publication may be reproduced, stored in a retrieval system or transmitted, in any form or by any means, electronic, mechanical, photocopying, recording or otherwise, without the prior written permission of the publisher. Printed in the United States of America.

Written by Jim Carrier, edited by Richard Cohen, research by the staff of the Intelligence Project

Design by Rodney Diaz and Russell Estes

FIGHT HATE

6 SPEAK UP

You, too, have First Amendment rights. Hate must be exposed and denounced. Buy an ad. Help news organizations achieve balance and depth. Do not debate hate mongers in conflict-driven talk shows.

7 LOBBY LEADERS

Persuade politicians, business and community leaders to take a stand against hate. Early action creates a positive reputation for the community, while unanswered hate will eventually be bad for business.

8 LOOK LONG RANGE

Create a "bias response" team. Hold annual events, such as a parade or culture fair, to celebrate your community's diversity and harmony. Build something the community needs. Create a Web site.

9 TEACH TOLERANCE

Bias is learned early, usually at home. But children from different cultures can be influenced by school programs and curricula. Sponsor an "I have a dream" contest. Target youths who may be tempted by skinheads or other hate groups.

10 DIG DEEPER

Look into issues that divide us: economic inequality, immigration, homosexuality. Work against discrimination in housing, employment, education. Look inside yourself for prejudices and stereotypes.

RESOURCES BEGIN ON PAGE 26
A COMPILATION OF ORGANIZATIONS AND MATERIALS THAT CAN ASSIST YOU IN FIGHTING HATE IN YOUR COMMUNITY

PHOTOGRAPHY CREDITS PAGE 28

TEN WAYS TO FIGHT HATE

1

ACT

DO SOMETHING. IN THE FACE OF HATRED, APATHY WILL BE INTERPRETED AS ACCEPTANCE — BY THE HATERS, THE PUBLIC AND, WORSE, THE VICTIM. DECENCY MUST BE EXERCISED, TOO. IF IT ISN'T, HATE INVARIABLY PERSISTS.

"THE KLAN IS COMING TO OUR TOWN. WHAT SHOULD we do?"

"I am very alarmed at hate crimes…What can I as Joe Citizen do to help?"

"I find myself wanting to act, to show support for the victims, to demonstrate my anger and sorrow…I don't know what to do, or how to begin…"

If you've opened this guide, you probably want to "do something" about hate. You are not alone. Queries like these arrive daily at the Southern Poverty Law Center. When a hate crime occurs or a hate group rallies, good people often feel helpless. We encourage you to act, for the following reasons:

• **Hate is an open attack on tolerance and decency.** It must be countered with acts of goodness. Sitting home with your virtue does no good. In the face of hate, silence is deadly. Apathy will be interpreted as acceptance — by the haters, the public and, worse, the victim. If not answered, hate can persist and grow.

• **Hate is an attack on a community's health.** It tears society along ethnic, gender and religious lines, and ignites emotions that need to be channeled. For all their "patriotic" rhetoric, hate groups and their freelance imitators are really trying to divide us. Their views are fundamentally anti-democratic. Your actions can support individual rights. Think of fighting hate as civil defense.

• **Hate events are rarely "isolated."** They often are a symptom of tension in the community. Take seriously even the smallest hint of hate — even name-calling. Those who are targeted do.

A SIXTH-GRADE CLASS in Morgantown, West Virginia, paints over skinhead graffiti on the outside wall of a convenience store. Their teacher used the graffiti to discuss hatred and violence.

YOU CAN:

• Pick up the phone. Call friends and colleagues. Host a small meeting. Stand up in church. Suggest some action.

• Sign a petition. Attend a vigil. Lead a prayer.

• Pick up a paint brush to cover graffiti.

• Use the skills and means you have. A San Diego musician wrote a song about the death of Matthew Shepard, the gay student in Laramie, Wyoming, and sold CDs to raise money for anti-hate groups. A Montana T-shirt shop printed up a shirt with a tolerance message. In Idaho, a plant manager bused employees to a rally denouncing white supremacists.

ONE PHONE CALL

When a cross was burned in the yard of a single mother of Portuguese descent in Rushville, Missouri, one person acted and set in motion a community uprising against hatred.

"I have been asked many times since that night why I got involved," said Christine Iverson. "The answer is simple. I was so upset after reading the article that I had to do something. So I got up and made a phone call. Everything else came from that moment of decision."

Iverson, a disaster response expert and pastor for Lutheran Social Services, called a friend involved in the church's anti-racism program. Then she called the victim. Then she called a ministerial alliance and asked to be put on the agenda. She went to the meeting with four proposals: a letter to the editor, a prayer meeting, flyer distribution and a candlelight vigil. The alliance recommended all four, and Iverson was put in charge.

The upshot was a gathering of 300 people, a speech by the mayor, news accounts of the rally, and the formation of a unity committee within the church alliance. Subsequently, over 150 people marched for the first time in a Martin Luther King Day parade, and an essay contest was created on the theme "We have a dream."

"There is still a lot of work to be done," said Iverson, "but we are beginning to do the work together."

IF I HAD A HAMMER

One of the easiest ways to get involved is to pick up a hammer. Painting over graffiti, replacing broken windows or building something together — sharing sweat equity — creates neighbors out of strangers and provides a tangible outlet that outlasts the emotion of the hate event. Like mini-monuments to tolerance, such projects become visible counterforces, pushing back against hate. They can spawn other projects and ongoing dialogue about divisive issues.

• One woman, Ammie Murray of Dixiana, South Carolina, is credited with rebuilding the tiny black-congregation St. John Baptist Church not once but twice after racist vandals destroyed it in 1985 and burned it to the ground in 1995. Discouraged and exhausted after the second incident and with continuous personal threats to her safety, the 65-year-old white woman nonetheless fired up a 1,000-person, multiracial work force that presented the congregation with a new church in November 1998.

• A sixth-grade class in Morgantown, West Virginia, painted over skinhead graffiti on the outside wall of a convenience store. Their teacher had used the graffiti to discuss hatred and violence. After watching "Not In Our Town," a video of how Billings, Montana, fought hate, the children concluded that, left to stand, the graffiti would convey community apathy. They became role models within Morgantown, with press coverage and congratulations from the state Attorney General.

• In the searing aftermath of the murder of James Byrd in Jasper, Texas, local black citizens reminded Jasper that the town swimming pool had been filled with dirt in the 1970s to prevent black children from integrating it. A mayor's task force proposed a new public pool.

• Reverberations from the Rodney King beating prompted the Los Angeles human relations commission to form neighborhood committees to pick building projects that would improve their multicultural neighborhoods. Years after the King incident, neighbors are designing and building flowerbeds, new stoplights and community centers.

• When a seven-foot cross was burned on the lawn of a young black couple in Kansas City, Kansas, it shocked neighbors. "They've just attacked the neighborhood," said a spokeswoman for the Rosedale Development Association. People from all over the city swarmed onto the property, repainting, replacing screens, mowing the yard, planting flowers. The victim hoped aloud that the perpetrator was watching, "so they can see that what they did backfired on them."

Pete Seeger, who, with Lee Hayes, wrote the song "If I Had a Hammer," says: "Hammers, shovels, picks, trowels, brushes, drills, wrenches — all are good tools. Let's all take a hammer...Let's find a way to build."

If the people of your town were armed with hammers, what would they build?

TEN WAYS TO FIGHT HATE

2 UNITE

CALL A FRIEND OR CO-WORKER. ORGANIZE A GROUP OF ALLIES FROM CHURCHES, SCHOOLS, CLUBS AND OTHER CIVIC SOURCES. CREATE A DIVERSE COALITION. INCLUDE CHILDREN, POLICE AND THE MEDIA. GATHER IDEAS FROM EVERYONE, AND GET EVERYONE INVOLVED.

YOUR INSTINCT FOR TOLERANCE IS SHARED BY OTHERS. There is power in numbers in the fight against hate. Asking for help and organizing a group reduces personal fear and vulnerability, spreads the workload and increases creativity and impact. Coalitions for tolerance can stand up to organized hate groups and isolate them. A group can act as a clearinghouse for information and establish a positive tone.

A hate crime often creates an opportunity for a community's first dialogue on race, homophobia or prejudice. It can help bridge the gap between neighborhoods and law enforcement. We think you'll be heartened by how many people want to act. As the creator of Project Lemonade (see story page 7) found, "There are plenty of people of good conscience out there."

FOUR CHILDREN meet at the first Community Cousins gathering in the wake of the Rodney King riots. From left, Tatiana Daniel, Drew Spiller, Quincy Bock, Sam Real.

IN THE BEGINNING:

- Call the circle around you: family, neighbors, co-workers, people in your church, synagogue or civic club. Meet informally at first.
- Call on groups that are likely to respond to a hate event: a faith alliance, labor unions, teachers, women's groups, university faculties, fair housing councils, the "Y" and youth groups. Make a special effort to involve businesses, politicians, police, children and members of minority and target groups.
- Go door-to-door in the neighborhood where the hate occurred, spreading the news and inviting participation in a rally, candlelight vigil or other public event. Put up ribbons or turn on porch lights as symbolic gestures. Declare a hate-free zone with a poster contest and a unity pledge. Set up a booth in a local mall to collect signatures on the pledge. Buy an ad and print the pledge and the contest winners.
- Fashion an appropriate, local response, but gather ideas from other towns that have faced hate events. A good starting point is a group viewing of the PBS video "Not in our Town." It tells the story of Billings, Montana's inspiring fight against white supremacists.

BIG STORIES/LITTLE SEEDS

Rodney King and Community Cousins

When four policemen were acquitted in 1992 of beating Rodney King, massive rioting and arson erupted in South Central Los Angeles. Hispanics, Blacks, Koreans and whites were plunged into one of the worst racial imbroglios in recent U.S. history. Up late with her newborn baby, Diane Bock of San Diego watched the live TV coverage in horror. "It kept weighing on me. How could you get people of different cultures to spend a little time together and stop stereotyping?" On that awful night, Community Cousins took shape. Bock, a marketer and former publisher, formed a nonprofit board, printed up brochures inviting participation and distributed them all over town. For an initial gathering, she hosted 39 families in her backyard with food and a puppet show and sign-up sheets to pair families with another from a different culture. She encouraged them to get together on their own and find ways to interact, such as swapping hand-me-down children's clothing. More than 200 families are now paired off. Periodically Bock holds group picnics, pumpkin carvings and swim parties. "It soaks into everything you do. It influences your children. No longer are you just talking to your kids about values. You're acting on your conviction. What you do counts 500 times more than what you say."

David Duke and Eracism

After David Duke's 1991 run for governor shook up Louisiana, *The Times-Picayune* of New Orleans published a massive series on race relations, "Together Apart," which included 1,000 letters and phone comments from readers.

Bookstore owner Rhoda Faust, a white woman, wrote: "Let's think of ways to let each other know that we love and respect one another as God's fellow creatures." Brenda Thompson, a black woman, called Faust. The two met for coffee and the group "Erace" was born. Their slogan, "Eracism – all colors with love and respect," is now carried on thousands of T-shirts and bumper stickers. The 200-member group sponsors regular, candid discussions on race. Said Faust: "Imagine a city where every car displays the sticker. Think of the message that would send. Think of how blacks and whites would feel in such a place."

Oklahoma City and a Living Memorial

America was still reeling from the April 19, 1995, explosion of the Murrah Building when Hunter Dupree, a relative of one of the victims and a retired historian, dropped a small seed in the smoking rubble. Dupree's cousin, Michael Thompson, had not even been found, nor the suspects or motives unearthed, when Dupree suggested at a family gathering that a "living" memorial — an institute to study terrorism — be built to honor the

PEACEFUL PROTESTERS stage a rally to counter a Ku Klux Klan rally in Franklin, Ohio.

dead. After Thompson's body was found, his brother, Toby, became active in a survivors' group. He subsequently helped write the mission statement for a national memorial. Toby Thompson remembered his cousin's suggestion and got it approved. The National Memorial Institute for the Prevention of Terrorism will be a public research facility across the street from the National Monument built on the site of the destroyed building. A memorial official says of the institute: "We can build the most beautiful memorial, but if we can't teach that terrorism is intolerable, we haven't completed our mission."

PROJECT LEMONADE

Bill and Lindy Seltzer, a Jewish couple in Springfield, Illinois, were frustrated that the First Amendment gave neo-Nazis the right to march in public rallies. So they devised an aikido approach to turn the tables on the haters and to turn their bitterness into something sweet. Project Lemonade, now used in dozens of communities, raises money for tolerance causes by collecting pledges for every minute of a hate-group event.

The Seltzers organized their first Project Lemonade during a 1994 Ku Klux Klan rally in Springfield. Using school equipment, they copied and mailed thousands of pledge flyers. Then they held a press conference to announce the unique event. They raised $10,000. When *People* magazine picked up the story, the idea spread nationwide.

The Seltzers made up a kit for other communities that included practical advice: "Schedule an organizational meeting with community leaders, arrange for a local telephone number and answering machine, recruit volunteers, raise seed money, carry a supply of cover letters and pass them out. Involve the police. Invite the media. Schedule press conferences. Try to be interviewed for radio and TV talk shows. Keep Project Lemonade in the media as much as possible."

Lindy also warned would-be organizers to expect hate calls. "Ignore them. Stay positive and respectful. Encourage people to stay away from the Klan rally. They are looking for a fight. The Klan will leave, and the community will have the last say. It will be a positive one."

As Projects Lemonade spread, the Seltzers estimated that, collectively, their pledges were raising $5,000 to $8,000 per minute. The money has gone to civil rights groups, including the Southern Poverty Law Center, the NAACP and local committees fighting hate, and for library books on civil rights and tolerance.

• In Coeur d'Alene, Idaho, the $28,000 raised during one supremacist rally will construct a Holocaust memorial in a city park. The plaque will credit the Aryan Nations for "making the memorial possible!"

• Coloradans United Against Hatred raises pledges to respond to future hate crimes and includes a pledge "card" on its Web site *www.cuah.org*. Half the money goes to victims, the other half to community programs such as sensitivity training for police.

• In Boyertown, Pennsylvania, Project Lemonade so irritated the Ku Klux Klan that the group threatened to sue organizers for raising money "on our name." Money raised went for library books on black history.

TEN WAYS TO FIGHT HATE

3 SUPPORT THE VICTIMS

HATE-CRIME VICTIMS ARE ESPECIALLY VULNERABLE, FEARFUL AND ALONE. LET THEM KNOW YOU CARE. SURROUND THEM WITH PEOPLE THEY FEEL COMFORTABLE WITH. IF YOU'RE A VICTIM, REPORT EVERY INCIDENT AND ASK FOR HELP.

VICTIMS OF HATE CRIMES FEEL TERRIBLY ALONE AND afraid. They have been attacked for being who they are, and silence amplifies their isolation. They need a strong, quick message that they are valued. Small acts of kindness — a phone call, a letter – can help.

• In Montgomery, Alabama, after hate mail and nails were thrown at black families in a formerly all-white neighborhood, a woman left a rose and a card, telling them "You are not alone."

• As white supremacists marched in Coeur d'Alene, Idaho, a number of families invited black and Hispanic neighbors to dinner. "Just as a way of saying, 'You are welcome,'" said one host.

• When the Inner City Church in Knoxville, Tennessee, was burned and spray-painted with racial threats, a local chapter of the National Coalition Building Institute gathered 300 signatures of support and presented them to the congregation as it met three days later in the parking lot.

A HATE CRIME ISN'T JUST "MISCHIEF"

A burning cross evokes for blacks the terrifying specter of lynching. A scrawled swastika is an epithet from the Holocaust that says Jews are not wanted alive. Because hate criminals target members of a group, an attack on one is meant as an attack on all, and the terror is felt by others in the group. We urge hate victims to report the crime to police. Because they may fear "the system," they may welcome the presence of others at the police station or courthouse.

• After white supremacists harassed a Sacramento family, a labor union provided round-the-clock security. At Gonzaga University in Spokane, administrators moved final exams for harassed black students to a safe location.

• When a cross was burned at a migrant camp in Bellingham, Washington, police hired a translator from the Immigration and Naturalization Service to gather information. Suddenly afraid of being deported, the migrant worker wouldn't talk, until a human rights worker interceded.

IF YOU ARE A VICTIM

Only you can decide whether to reveal your identity. But many victims have found the courage to lend their names to fighting hate. If you decide to speak up, we recommend:

• Reporting every incident. If you are a targeted minority, harassment could continue. What began as egg throwing at five black families in rural Selbrook, Alabama, escalated for 18 months until hate mail made it a federal offense. The story made the news, police patrolled and harassment declined.

• Speaking to the press. Your story, with a frank discussion of the impact on your family life, can be a powerful motivator to others. Copycat crimes are possible, but rare. More likely, you'll be encouraged by love and support. After an Arab-American family in Montgomery County, Maryland, was repeatedly harassed during the Gulf War, the mother told her story. The community rallied, and a suspect was convicted. In Watertown, New York, a black minister

talked about the vulgar hate mail he received. His community held a special unity rally. "Denying that racism exists, or not talking about it, will not cause it to go away," he said.

• Researching your legal rights. After enduring racial slurs, slashed tires, broken windows, and the wounding of their dog by their white neighbor, a six-foot burning cross finally moved Andrew Bailey and Sharon Henderson of Chicago to file suit against the neighbor. A federal jury awarded them $720,000.

NOT IN OUR TOWN

Christmas was just around the corner in 1993 when Billings, Montana, entered a white supremacist hell. Jewish graves were vandalized. Native American homes were sprayed with epithets like "Die Indian." Skinheads harassed a black church congregation. But these events received scant notice — until 5-year-old Isaac Schnitzer's holiday peace was shattered.

On Dec. 2, a chunk of cinder block broke his upstairs window. The window displayed a menorah, a row of candles lighted at Hanukkah. Responding police urged his mother, Tammie Schnitzer, to take down all their Jewish symbols. She refused and said so boldly in a news story. She even urged front-page play.

As if suddenly aware of hate in its midst, Billings responded. Vigils were held. Petitions were signed. A painter's union led 100 people in repainting houses. Within days, the town erupted in menorahs — purchased at K-mart, Xeroxed in church offices and printed in the *Billings Gazette* — displayed in thousands of windows. Supremacists went crazy, throwing rocks, shooting out windows, killing a cat with an arrow. "Billings understood that it had a war on its hands," *The New York Times* later noted. Still, Mrs. Schnitzer took her son for a ride through town to look at all the menorahs.

"Are they Jewish, too?" a wide-eyed Isaac asked.

"No," she said, "they're friends."

The manager of a local sporting goods store, Rick Smith, was so moved by events that he changed the sales pitch on his street marquee. Instead of an ad for school letter jackets, he mounted, in foot-high letters: "Not in Our Town. No Hate. No Violence. Peace on Earth." The marquee got national exposure and "Not in Our Town" became a famous slogan. It went on to title a Hollywood movie, a PBS special and a tolerance movement in more than 30 states.

Not in Our Town, with its forceful message to hate groups, is now spread by The Working Group, a nonprofit production company that produced the video, "Not In Our Town." Subsequent videos show what communities around the country have done to fight hate.

ACTING BEFORE A HATE INCIDENT, Rockford, Illinois, organized a "Not in Our Town" rally to focus attention on intergroup tension. Supporters signed a proclamation to oppose bigotry, correct discrimination and promote tolerance.

TEN WAYS TO FIGHT HATE

4 DO YOUR HOMEWORK

DETERMINE IF A HATE GROUP IS INVOLVED, AND RESEARCH ITS SYMBOLS AND AGENDA. SEEK ADVICE FROM ANTI-HATE ORGANIZATIONS. ACCURATE INFORMATION CAN THEN BE SPREAD TO THE COMMUNITY.

KNOW WHO AND WHAT YOU'RE fighting. Eruptions of hate generally produce one of two reactions: apathy ("it's just an isolated act of kooks") or fear ("the world is out of control"). Before reacting, communities need accurate information about haters and their danger.

The Southern Poverty Law Center reports nearly 700 organized U.S. hate groups, virtually all white supremacists with a handful of black separatist groups. Some are tiny — a handful of men — but armed with a computer, E-mail and a Web site, their reach is immense, their message capable of entering a child's private bedroom.

KU KLUX KLAN MEMBERS give a white power salute at a rally outside the Statehouse in Columbus, Ohio.

In their literature and Web sites, hate groups rail at growing minority populations that will make whites another minority in the 21st century. Like some of their brothers-in-arms in militia groups, they also spread fears of losing control of America to a "One World Government" dominated by Jewish bankers, multinational corporations and the United Nations. More often than not, members of hate groups use scapegoats to blame for their personal failures, low self-esteem, anger and frustration. They frequently act under the influence of alcohol or drugs.

Though their views may be couched in code words, members of hate groups typically share these extremist views:
• They want to limit the rights of certain groups and separate society along racial, ethnic or religious lines.
  • They believe in conspiracies.
  • They try to silence any opposition.
  • They are antigovernment and fundamentalist.

And yet, most hate crimes are not committed by members of hate groups. SPLC estimates that less than 5 percent of hate crimes can be linked to group members. The majority appear to be the work of "free-lance" haters, young males who are looking for thrills, or defending some turf, or trying to blame someone for their troubles. Rarely are they acting from deeply held ideology. These young men have adopted the rhetoric of hate groups, however, and they mix stereotypes with a culture of violence. In their minds, certain people are "suitable victims," somehow deserving of their hostility. They attack target groups randomly, choosing whoever is convenient.

GET HELP FROM EXPERTS

The Southern Poverty Law Center, the Anti-Defamation League and many other human rights organizations have information and advice on hate groups. They have helped many communities deal with crises.

• When skinheads threatened to disrupt the performance of a punk band with a human rights message, Eugene, Oregon, panicked and canceled the concert. "The neo-Nazi skinheads won," said Eric Ward, co-director of the University of Oregon's black student union at the time. "None of us knew anything about the white supremacist movement." Ward helped form a group, Communities Against Hate, and sent for literature from the Southern Poverty Law Center. "I remember reading my first *Klanwatch Report* and feeling sick to my stomach." The group then gathered data on local skinheads and, when several individuals fired a machine gun into a Jewish synagogue, provided police with tips that led to an arrest. When skinheads began following students of color home from school, the group called a forum and showed slides of 40 Nazis living in Salem, 60 miles away. The skinheads were identified with brutal frankness: "This guy took an ice pick to a Hispanic...this Nazi took a knife and stabbed Stephen at this school," said Michele Lefkowith of Communities Against Hate.

• When a white power rock concert was announced in Traverse City, Michigan, a group of citizens created "Hate-Free TC" and sought help from the Center for New Community. In a day-long seminar, human rights experts educated local people about neo-Nazi skinheads, their racist music and their connection to an international movement that includes Nazis, white supremacists and the Christian Identity church. They later held an alternative rock concert, and the publicity forced cancellation of the white power gathering.

• After seeing mail, including a "pastor's license," arrive for his son, an Indiana father realized that the teenager was connecting to a hate Web site operated by a white supremacist group guised as a church. It helped explain the boy's adoption of Nazi symbols and style. The father wrote the church, demanded that E-mail be stopped and threatened suit.

TALE OF TWO PENNSYLVANIA TOWNS

Pennsylvania became a hotbed of Ku Klux Klan activity in the 1990s in the wake of widespread economic decline. Two small, white, rural communities, on opposite ends of the state, took fundamentally different tacks when faced with men in sheets on their streets.

BOYERTOWN

This picturesque village of 3,000 people, antique stores and country homes 50 miles from Philadelphia awoke one Saturday in the autumn of 1988 to find eight men in white KKK robes standing at a downtown intersection, handing out literature. They were quiet and polite, and the town, while abuzz, tried to ignore them.

Ten years later, in the fall of 1998, the masked Klansman were still at the intersection of Philadelphia and Reading Avenues, their presence having become so routine that one journalist described them as "regular street corner evangelists." By then, a white supremacist was advising the school board, and Klan members were distributing door-to-door hate fliers that showed a black man in chains scrawled with epithets.

When Ann Van Dyke of Pennsylvania's Human Relations Commission urged the city officials to denounce the Klan, they declined. "They are not bothering anybody," they told her. "We want to be neutral."

In the vacuum, a small group of residents formed the Boyertown Unity Coalition. They studied material about the Klan leaders and interviewed former white supremacists. On Martin Luther King Jr.'s birthday, they solicited statements of tolerance from businesses and churches and printed them in a newspaper ad. They also collected $8,000 in Project Lemonade pledges for tolerance library books. After two summers of the Lemonade pledges, town fathers remained mum, but the coalition attracted 400 people to a Martin Luther King Jr. birthday celebration. "In a town that harbored the Klan, here's 400 people showing up," said coalition founder Phil Donnelly. "To me that's showing we're gaining."

YUKON

Thirty hilly miles outside of Pittsburgh, the village of Yukon, population 700, has been home to coal miners for generations. It also contains a toxic industrial dump that many suspect of poisoning animals and humans. Yukon was astonished in the summer of 1997 when the Ku Klux Klan announced plans to buy a farm next to the dump, "take on" the dump's corporate owner and create a paramilitary training center.

As the Klan announced its first major rally, local minister Chris Boucher asked for help from the Pennsylvania Human Relations Commission. He then organized a "Yukon United" picnic and half the town showed up. "Why a picnic? Western Pennsylvania is a melting pot. One thing we can all come together around is food." Between music and burgers and fire squad demonstrations, people were encouraged to tell their family immigration histories, which subtly made the point that Yukon had always been a town of newcomers. The media gave the picnic great play, compared to the racial epithets blared by the Klan at its rally.

Under the banner of "Not Hate Not Here," Yukon United held vigils at the edge of the farm as Klan members jackbooted around. Klan attendance diminished, Klan members trashed the farm and no effort was made to clean up the dump. Finally, the property owner kicked them off. Said Boucher: "The Klan found they weren't going to sign up people and generate the interest they'd hoped for."

TEN WAYS TO FIGHT HATE

5

CREATE AN ALTERNATIVE

DO NOT ATTEND A HATE RALLY. FIND ANOTHER OUTLET FOR ANGER AND FRUSTRATION AND PEOPLE'S DESIRE TO DO SOMETHING. HOLD A UNITY RALLY OR PARADE. FIND A NEWS HOOK, LIKE A "HATE-FREE ZONE."

Hate has a First Amendment right. Courts have routinely upheld the constitutional right of the Ku Klux Klan and other hate groups to hold rallies and say what they want. In 1998, for example, the American Knights of the Ku Klux Klan held 39 weekend rallies in 14 states. Communities can restrict group movements to avoid conflicts with other citizens, but hate rallies will continue. Your efforts should focus on channeling people away from rallies.

DO NOT ATTEND A HATE RALLY

As much as you'd like to physically show your opposition to hate, shout back or throw something, confrontations only serve the haters. They also burden law enforcement with protecting hate mongers against otherwise law-abiding citizens.

• In Memphis, Tennessee, a riot broke out between a Klan rally and counter-demonstrators on Martin Luther King's birthday. More than 100 police threw tear gas canisters and arrested 20 anti-Klan demonstrators while protecting the Klan's right to rally and speak.

• A 25-minute march by the Aryan Nations through 15 blocks of Coeur d'Alene, Idaho, cost the state, county and city more than $125,000 for public safety. Mayor Steve Judy described this as money spent to protect free speech. "But we could have taken the money and done a lot for human rights with it."

• Ann Arbor, Michigan, was stung by a 1996 rally in which 300 police failed to protect the Klan from a chanting crowd that threw rocks and sticks, hurting seven policemen and destroying property. The Klan's members were able to stand on the First Amendment, surrounded by what one of their leaders called "animal behavior." Two years later, Ann Arbor police were better prepared. A 115-person "peace team" was trained to stand between the Klan and its opponents. Anti-Klan forces tore down a fence and police again used tear gas, but commentators felt the yellow-shirted peace team kept trouble to a minimum. The team remained together for rapid response to hate events.

A WORLD OF IDEAS

Every act of hatred should be met with an act of love and unity. Many communities facing a Klan rally have held alternative events at the same hour, some distance away. They have included a community picnic, a parade or unity fair with food, music, exhibits and entertainment. These events emphasize strength in diversity and the positive

CAUZETTA POWELL, standing, and a woman who asked to remain unidentified, sing at a unity rally in Jasper, Texas, following the dragging death of James Byrd Jr.

aspects of the community. They also give people a safe outlet for the frustration and anger they want to vent. As a woman at a Spokane human rights rally and reggae dance put it, "Being passive is something I don't want to do. I need to make some kind of commitment to human rights."

• After the dragging death of James Byrd Jr. in Jasper, Texas, the KKK rallied on the courthouse lawn while black Muslims paraded by. Local people, who had demonstrated their feelings at a courthouse vigil one week after the murder, stayed away. Yellow ribbons from that event still fluttered from locked storefronts as a mute response to the Klan's hate. Hundreds of journalists did record the black-versus-white demonstrations, but locals were not involved.

• Pulaski, Tennessee, the birthplace of the Ku Klux Klan in 1866, closed its doors to white supremacists attempting to rally in 1989. Racists found the town closed for business, including McDonald's, the grocery store and Wal-Mart. "They couldn't find a place to get a hamburger or even go to the bathroom," the mayor said. In subsequent years, the KKK rally became a joke, and even the media got bored with it. "Last year no one came," said the mayor, "The year before that, the only TV was the Comedy Channel."

• When the Klan came to Indianapolis, local museums, the state capitol and other attractions opened their doors to citizens for free. Community leaders held a youth rally in a ballroom. A huge coalition, including the mayor and the NFL's Indianapolis Colts, placed a full-page ad in *The Indianapolis Star* deploring the Klan.

• During a unity parade in a Pennsylvania village, a local clown troupe donned red noses, wigs and floral sheets under the name Kook Lutz Klowns to spoof the fascists. In Pittsburgh, a coalition held a "parade of banners" in which families carried homemade banners with a message either denouncing hate or promoting diversity.

• When the Klan rallied in Madison, Wisconsin, a coalition of ministers organized citizens to spend the day working in minority homes and neighborhoods. Volunteer Judy Dettwiler said she wanted to "do something constructive and uplifting which would be in opposition to what the Klan stands for. So, I'm cleaning cupboards at the Hispanic community center this afternoon. I've never been there, but I'm looking forward to doing something for my community."

• When the Ku Klux Klan announced plans to clean up shoulders and ditches along a stretch of road under the Adopt-a-Highway program in Palatine, Illinois — and officials realized they couldn't stop it — local teenagers flooded City Hall with so many applications that they claimed every inch of highway earmarked for the program and pushed the Klan onto a waiting list. "Truth and love and kindness and caring won out over hate," Mayor Rita Mullins said. "It restored my faith in humanity."

• For many years in Cincinnati, the KKK has erected a cross and rallied in the downtown Fountain Square at Christmas. Embarrassed city officials failed to stop it in court so decided to keep a low profile, fearing bad publicity. But when Klan attendance appeared to be growing, City Councilman Tyrone Yates organized a multicultural flashlight vigil on an evening when Klan members would not be around. Speakers included national civil rights heroes. "You couldn't let the evil of the Klan cross just stand there with no voice in opposition," said Yates. "Too few speak out because it is uneasy, it is uncomfortable, it is inconvenient and it may ruin our shopping season," he told a local reporter. "But in the long run we help our cause and we help our downtown."

TEN WAYS TO FIGHT HATE

6 SPEAK UP

YOU, TOO, HAVE FIRST AMENDMENT RIGHTS. HATE MUST BE EXPOSED AND DENOUNCED. BUY AN AD. HELP NEWS ORGANIZATIONS ACHIEVE BALANCE AND DEPTH. DO NOT DEBATE HATE MONGERS IN CONFLICT-DRIVEN TALK SHOWS.

GOODNESS HAS A FIRST AMENDMENT RIGHT, TOO. WE urge you to denounce hate groups and hate crimes, and spread the truth about hate's threat to a pluralistic society. An informed community is the best defense against hate.

You can spread tolerance through church bulletins, door-to-door flyers, Web sites, local cable TV bulletin boards, letters to the editor and print advertisements. Hate shrivels under strong light. Beneath their neo-Nazi exteriors, hate purveyors are cowards, surprisingly subject to public pressure and ostracism.

THOUSANDS ATTENDED a rally in New York City to honor Matthew Shepard, a gay man murdered in Laramie, Wyoming.

• When the 20-year-old "national leader" of the Aryan Nations in Canada was exposed by the *Prince George Citizen*, he resigned and closed his Web site. "I don't want to have this plastered all over the place," he said.

• Floyd Cochran, a former recruiter for the Aryan Nations, recalls the night he and founder Richard Butler traveled to tiny Sandpoint, Idaho, to intimidate a human relations meeting. When they found 300 people, they were intimidated themselves. "I didn't go back to Sandpoint because of the turnout," Cochran said.

DEALING WITH MEDIA

• News outlets cover hate crimes and groups. Don't kill the messenger. Consider hate news a wake-up call, revealing tension in the community. Attack the problem. Reporters will then cover you, too.

• Name a press contact for your group. This keeps the message consistent and allows the press to quickly seek comment or reaction to events. Invite the press to all your meetings.

• The media likes news hooks and catchy phrases like "Hate free zone." Propose human-interest stories, such as the impact of hate on individuals. Think of "photo-ops." Kids make good subjects.

• Educate reporters, editors and publishers about hate groups, their symbols and their effect on victims and communities. Put them in touch with hate experts like the Southern Poverty Law Center. Urge editorial stands against hate.

• Criticize the press when it falls short. Remind editors that it is not fair to focus on 20 Klansmen when 300 people attend a peace rally.

• Do not debate white supremacists or other hate mongers on conflict-driven talk shows or public forums. Your presence lends them legitimacy and publicity, they use code words to cover their hate beliefs, and they misinterpret history and Bible verses in a manner that is difficult to counter under time constraints.

TO THE MEDIA

There is a relationship between your coverage of race and race relations in your market. A newsroom that covers race issues thoroughly and regularly sets an agenda for the community. Though sometimes ugly to view, the venting of intergroup tensions through your stories and letters serves as a release valve.

Take hate crimes seriously and display them prominently. Consider an annual "race report card." Give reporters time to cover the Klan and other hate groups in depth, beyond the annual parade. Don't miss the "good news" as ordinary people struggle with home-grown ways to promote tolerance. Cover the impact of hate on victims and other members of target groups. Become an activist against hate, just as you are against crime. Sponsor a forum or other community journalism event. Sponsor a contest for the best tolerance ad from local agencies and publish or broadcast the winner.

THE REV. DAVID OSTENDORF leads a prayer vigil at the East Peoria, Illinois, home of Matt Hale, leader of the racist World Church of the Creator. Days before, a Hale disciple killed two and wounded nine, before killing himself.

COVERING THE KKK

A Ku Klux Klan rally makes for wonderful photos. A cross burning draws cameras like moths to flames. Consider these points:

• The masked, mysterious Klansman, like his burning cross, is an emotional, even thrilling, image loaded with associations from a dark history. Don't let this cliché control the story or prevent coverage of deeper issues. Include a serious look at the Klan's numbers and influence, its involvement in hate crimes, and the hypocrisy of its pseudo-Christian message.

• Consider the Klan's effect, and the power of hate images, on people of color. A hooded Klansman on TV or front page exaggerates and extends the Klan's reach. You wouldn't carry an ad for a terrorist act, but an uncritical story amounts to the same thing. Attempt to make a tolerance photo with equal emotion.

• Don't allow hate groups to masquerade as white-pride civic groups. In their literature and Web sites, they denigrate certain scapegoats, including minorities. Consult local police, state human rights commissions, the Intelligence Project of the Southern Poverty Law Center or the research office of the Anti-Defamation League.

• Klan and other white supremacist rallies are the prototypical media event. They represent good versus evil. But their demagoguery represents the outer margin of American society. No meaningful dialogue on race can occur when it is played so black and white.

THE TIMES PICAYUNE: THEN & NOW

The ascendance of former Ku Klux Klansman David Duke to a runoff election for governor of Louisiana was a shock to the nation. At *The Times-Picayune*, New Orleans' daily newspaper, it was a slap in the face. The paper had covered Duke's early political career conservatively, fearing too much coverage of an extremist point of view. But during the four-week runoff campaign between Duke and former governor Edwin Edwards, the newspaper pulled out the stops, aggressively covering and editorializing against Duke's white supremacist views and his likely impact on Louisiana. "What was at stake was the survival of the state," said Editor Jim Amoss. After Edwards won, Amoss said, the newspaper asked itself, "What fueled this incredible movement. What are we missing here?" The result was a massive series on race in 1993 that riveted the city and changed the nature of the race debate in New Orleans.

"Together Apart: The Myth of Race" covered virtually every story one could think of about race, including slavery, genetics, intelligence, discrimination, segregation and attitudes. The most remarkable feature was 53 pages of reader reaction, many anonymous and ugly. More than 6,500 people called in comments, and 1,000 were printed. The paper initially lost 1,000 subscribers because of the series. But by the end of the series, readers were writing and calling responses to other reader comments. "It became a dialogue among readers, a great thing, talking with honesty you don't often see in newspaper pages," said Amoss.

More than anything, the series gave New Orleans the vocabulary and license to talk openly about race, especially across racial lines. The newsroom became more diverse and open, as well, which had the rippling effect of better, fairer and deeper coverage of the ongoing race story in New Orleans.

TEN WAYS TO FIGHT HATE

7 LOBBY LEADERS

PERSUADE POLITICIANS, BUSINESS AND COMMUNITY LEADERS TO TAKE A STAND AGAINST HATE. EARLY ACTION CREATES A POSITIVE REPUTATION FOR THE COMMUNITY, WHILE UNANSWERED HATE WILL EVENTUALLY BE BAD FOR BUSINESS.

STEVE OSTERLUND, carrying Victoria Elliott, 4, walks with Anna Duncan and Rev. Kenneth Elliott (Victoria's dad) during a "unity march" to celebrate Martin Luther King Jr. Day in Spokane, Washington.

THE FIGHT AGAINST HATE NEEDS COMMUNITY LEADERS willing to take a stand. Mayor, police chief, college president, school principal, corporate CEO: key people can quickly turn a hate event into a positive community experience. They can muster support. They are quoted in the news. They set a tone, direction and good example. Without leadership, much of the public, busy with raising children and changing channels, will continue to avoid the issue.

Silence from a leader creates a vacuum. Rumors spread and victims and perpetrators get the wrong message. Since Hitler's Germany, silence has been recognized as hate's greatest ally. The lesson was relearned in the 1980s and 1990s in many American states faced with the new white supremacists and militia groups. Fear of "negative publicity" resulted in silence. In many cases, hate escalated and became not just a public relations nightmare, but also a deadly threat to individuals and the civic order.

WE RECOMMEND:

• **A quick, serious police response to hate crimes.** Vigorous prosecution also encourages the public to stand up against hate.

• **A strong public statement by political leaders.** Politically, there is no "down side" to a public stand against hate, and official opposition intimidates members of hate groups. The mayor of Albuquerque, New Mexico, for example, signed an official proclamation declaring a hate group "to be un-welcome in our city." In Wisconsin, the Dane

County board issued a strongly worded official condemnation of the KKK prior to a rally.

• **A working relationship between police and human rights coalitions.** When police are called and determine a hate crime, they should notify coalitions. Victim support can begin immediately. In return, coalitions can act as early warning systems for law enforcement. Montgomery County, Maryland, sponsors a hot line for reporting crimes, with rewards for tips leading to an arrest.

TOLERANCE ON THE JOB

The workplace in America is an untapped resource for promoting tolerance. Adults of all sexes, races, religions and ethnicities mix for long hours in pursuit of a common goal. We urge CEOs to turn this force loose on both the bottom line and community problems.

• Proctor & Gamble has funded television ads, "Don't Be Afraid, Be a Friend," that encourage children to make friends across racial, ethnic and disability lines.

• Levi Strauss contributed $5 million to Project Change to reduce racial prejudice and hate crimes and to help people of color get loans in communities where it has plants: Knoxville, Albuquerque, El Paso and Valdosta, Georgia.

• The Greater Seattle Chamber of Commerce sponsors "It's Time to Talk" to encourage business professionals to share personal experiences across race lines. After an annual banquet, the chamber coordinates hundreds of integrated dinner parties in private homes.

• The White Dog Café in Philadelphia uses "good food to lure customers into social activism," says founder Judy Wicks, who began a "sister restaurant" program in the city's ghetto areas. She escorts upscale white customers out for dinner at minority-owned restaurants followed by ethnic programs ranging from Latino dance clubs to black theater. Ten percent of the company's profits go into social activism.

THE PRICE OF SILENCE

IDAHO'S IMAGE

People laughed when a former aerospace engineer named Richard Butler bought 20 acres in Hayden Lake, north of Coeur d'Alene, in the 1970s and announced plans for an "Aryan Nation." His marches and diatribes were carried in the news, but they seemed preposterous and he was dismissed as another kook in the woods.

Looking back, it is easy to follow the escalation from words to deeds, from demagoguery to crimes: A gathering of neo-Nazis. A swastika scrawled on a Jewish-owned restaurant. A threat to biracial children. Firebombing of the home of a Coeur d'Alene priest. The murder of talk show host Alan Berg. Bank robberies. Explosions at a federal building and an abortion clinic.

Bill Wassmuth, the former priest whose home was bombed, heads the Northwest Coalition Against Malicious Harassment. He lists 21 examples of how racist and extremist groups have made the area "their home." Among them: the opening of a Christian Identity bookstore in Hayden, a survivalists' expo in Spokane, a militia that trains with live ammo, and the woods full of hate purveyors who show up at town meetings, spray graffiti and mail hate videos and posters to neighbors.

More than 100 grass-roots human rights groups have formed in Idaho to fight this activity. But tolerance leaders say hate is entrenched and shows no sign of stopping.

CORPORATE RECRUITING IN A STATE OF HATE

Hewlett Packard makes its popular laser-jet printer in one of the most beautiful sites in the country, but when it tries to recruit workers, they ask about the Aryan Nations, says Cindy Stanphill, the company's diversity and staffing manager. "And it's not just people of color. People tell us, if the state allows that to go on, that's not where I want my kids raised, in a state where hate is allowed to have a voice." As a result, she says, HP loses many good people. Attrition rates for people of color are double the average.

HP's frankness about Idaho comes after failing to live up to its corporate goal of diversity. After a self examination, HP decided that its recruiting woes were not due to a poor "image" so much as deeply rooted attitudes within the community and the plant's workforce.

In 1998, HP-Idaho began practicing tolerance. It produced a TV commercial shown during the final Seinfeld show. It held rock "diversity" concerts. It has sponsored a symposium in which minority people told their stories. On Martin Luther King's birthday, HP bused employees to rallies. The division president spoke on the Capitol steps and testified in favor of adding sexual orientation to the state's hate crime act. Said Stanphill: "Our commitment comes from the fundamental belief that everyone wants to do a good job, and, given the right environment, they will do a good job and we will be successful."

TEN WAYS TO FIGHT HATE

8

LOOK LONG RANGE

CREATE A "BIAS RESPONSE" TEAM. HOLD ANNUAL EVENTS, SUCH AS A PARADE OR CULTURE FAIR, TO CELEBRATE YOUR COMMUNITY'S DIVERSITY AND HARMONY. BUILD SOMETHING THE COMMUNITY NEEDS. CREATE A WEB SITE.

THE ONLY RULE at The Friendly Supper Club monthly meeting in Montgomery, Alabama, is to bring a guest of another race.

THE BEST BARRIER TO HATE IS A TOLERANT COMMUNITY. After a hate crisis, we recommend turning a crisis team into a long-term tolerance committee. A small group of committed people can build a moral barrier to hate or at least create an atmosphere in which hate outbreaks are rare. As Chris Boucher of Yukon, Pennsylvania, put it after a handful of people ran the Klan out of town: "A united coalition is like Teflon. Hate can't stick there."

Experts say the first step in changing hearts is to change behavior. By acting tolerant, people begin to respect one another. Begin with positive statements and symbolic gestures. Make tolerance a habit, an activity as normal as your kids' soccer practice.

VIGILS, DREAMS AND GOOD FOOD

• Hold candlelight vigils, religious services and other activities to bring people of different races, religions and ethnic groups together. In Boise, Idaho, Martin Luther King's birthday has become an 11-day Human Rights Celebration.

• Create a local "I Have a Dream" contest, in which people imagine and describe an ideal community. In North Berkshire, Massachusetts, winning essays by children are reproduced and rolled onto highway billboards donated by the Callahan Outdoor Advertising Company.

• Use any excuse to celebrate diversity. In Selma, Alabama, a major weekend street fair is held on the anniversary of Bloody Sunday, when voting-rights activists attempting to walk across a bridge to Montgomery were beaten back by police. In Denver, Cinco de Mayo has become a major celebration of Mexican culture.

• Break bread together. The Friendly Supper Club in Montgomery, Alabama, has no agenda, no speakers and only one rule at its monthly meeting: bring a person of another race or culture with you for "honest interaction."

• Move from prayer to action: In California's San Fernando Valley, an interfaith council has formed "home dialogues" with men and women from different faiths and cultures who meet together in their homes. In Covington, Kentucky, churchwomen conducted a letter-writing campaign to support hate crime legislation. They later promoted teacher training in race relations.

• Begin a community conversation on race. Discussion groups, book clubs, Internet chat rooms and library gatherings can bring people together. One of the most effective sessions allows individuals to tell their stories, their immigration history, their daily encounters with discrimination, their fear about revealing sexual orientation.

• Consider building something the community needs, from Habitat for Humanity housing to a new park.

• Create a tolerance Web site. Coloradans United Against Hate is a Web-based, "paperless organization" with a virtual billboard that posts stories and comments on local hate issues.

TOLERANCE NETWORKS

Many regions have created networks of human rights coalitions. They share information on hate groups and individual hate mongers and can mobilize a large anti-hate team when needed.

The Michigan Ecumenical Forum, for example, organized a web of churches in Muskegon County after the Oklahoma City bombing revealed a connection to the Michigan militia movement. Taking stock, the Forum's mainstream churches realized that "a lot of good church folks" had become estranged from government, making them susceptible to militia recruitment, said Steven Johns Boehme, who heads the Forum.

The Forum sponsored a major conference on the militia. At its conclusion, participants created Community United for Peace, a county-wide clearinghouse for prejudice, race and hate issues and a bridge between villages and groups, between black and white churches. The coalition also acts as a nerve center, picking up news of white supremacist events throughout rural Michigan. The coalition has won accolades from the National Council of Churches.

"You have to stop thinking of the militia as wackos on the fringe," said Boehme. "They are there because the ground in the area is receptive for it. If you drop the seeds of prejudice in soil that is not receptive, they won't take root."

• The Pennsylvania Network of Unity Coalitions connects many groups that are fighting the Ku Klux Klan and other white supremacists throughout the state. The state publishes a "Klanwatch" list of activities. As hate groups test the waters of new communities with speeches and rallies, local leaders can call on the coalition's members for practical advice. Each new Klan rally tends to create a new local unity coalition, adding to the tolerance web.

• The Northwest Coalition against Malicious Harassment links grassroots groups in the hate hotbed of Montana, Idaho, Washington and Oregon. "No individual stands alone," says Director Bill Wassmuth, who believes local coalitions are the best single weapon against hate crimes. "You can create an atmosphere in which a bigot cannot thrive."

HATE NEXT DOOR

In Sandpoint, Idaho, fighting hate has become a daily exercise against hate mongers who happen to be neighbors. Once described by *GQ* magazine as the "Heart of Whiteness," Sandpoint, population 5,200, is in the geographic center of a self-declared anti-government, white supremacist "homeland." Praised nationally for beating back an initial wave of bias, a local coalition has been forced to dig in for the long haul.

The Bonner County Human Rights Committee was established in 1992 after the Aryan Nations tried to recruit locally. Members of the committee went door to door for support and drew 300 people to a meeting. In 1995, the committee flooded the area with child-designed holiday cards carrying messages of racial harmony.

But after a first round of positive publicity, people of Sandpoint were stunned by the sudden arrival in their mail of anti-Semitic booklets, six-foot posters asserting the superiority of whites, videotapes and racist comic books. Booklets were even left on windshields of churchgoers. The blitzkrieg was the work of Carl Story and Vincent Bertollino, right-wing millionaires who settled in Sandpoint and spent $1.5 million in one year spreading hate material.

In response, the coalition established an Emergency Hate Response Kit, which includes suggestions on how to respond, tolerance bumper stickers and window posters on human rights. For fun they added a list of the Top 10 ways to recycle racist literature.

"There's a lot at stake here," said Sandpoint Mayor David Sawyer. "It's more than image. It's more than an abrasive act that happens every once in a while. It's the quality of the atmosphere of this town."

TEN WAYS TO FIGHT HATE 9

TEACH TOLERANCE

BIAS IS LEARNED EARLY, USUALLY AT HOME. BUT CHILDREN FROM DIFFERENT CULTURES CAN BE INFLUENCED BY SCHOOL PROGRAMS AND CURRICULA. SPONSOR AN "I HAVE A DREAM" CONTEST. TARGET YOUTHS WHO MAY BE TEMPTED BY SKINHEADS OR OTHER HATE GROUPS.

BIAS IS LEARNED IN CHILDHOOD. BY THE age of three, children are aware of racial differences and may have the perception that "white" is desirable. By the age of 12, they hold stereotypes about numerous ethnic, racial and religious groups, according to the Leadership Conference Education Fund. Because stereotypes underlie hate, and almost half of all hate crimes are committed by young men under 20, tolerance education is critical.

About 10 percent of hate crimes occur in schools and colleges, but schools can be an ideal environment to counter bias. Schools mix youths of different backgrounds, place them on equal footings and allow one-on-one interaction. Children are also naturally curious about people who are different.

Teaching Tolerance, a program of the Southern Poverty Law Center, believes that diversity education should begin in preschool and continue through college.

CLASSROOM ACTIVITIES FOR PROMOTING TOLERANCE

• Acknowledge differences among students and celebrate the uniqueness of every one. In Debra Goldsbury's first-grade class in Seattle, children paint self-portraits, mixing colors to match their skin tone. They then name their colors, which have included "gingerbread," "melon" and "terra cotta." They learn that everyone has a color, that no one is actually "white."

• Establish a "You can't say you can't play" policy. Created by teacher Vivian Paley in Chicago, the rule prohibits the kind of hurtful rejection children dish out and suffer. "We must start in kindergarten," she says. "Justice must become an intuitive law."

• Promote inclusion and fairness, but allow discussions of all feelings, including bias learned at home and the street. Establish a "peace table" where children learn to "fight fair," perhaps with hand puppets in which conflict is acted out.

LEARNING TOGETHER: Nancy Lepiato, left, and Kristin Wheeler are students at Robert M. Lusher elementary, a New Orleans school with nearly equal numbers of black and white students.

• Use sports to bridge racial gaps. In Brooklyn, New York, an interracial basketball program called Flames was founded in the mid-'70s. Since then it has brought together more than 10,000 young people of diverse backgrounds.

• Promote diversity by letting children tell stories about their families, however different they may be. Diversity embraces not just race, but age, religion, marital status and personal ability. Remember that charting "family trees" can be a challenge to some children, such as those who are adopted or living with single parents.

• Teach older children to look critically at stereotypes portrayed by the media. Ask them to close their eyes and imagine a lawyer, doctor, rap musician, gang member, bank president, hair stylist or criminal. What did they "see" and why? Confronted with their own stereotypes, children begin to question how they've been shaped by the media.

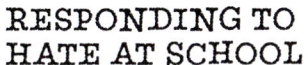

• Teach mediation skills to kids. Some 300,000 high school students are physically attacked every month, by some estimates. One survey of 130 New York City teachers found that after student mediators went to work, incidents of violence and name calling declined dramatically, while cooperation and communication among students increased significantly.

RESPONDING TO HATE AT SCHOOL

The massacre at Columbine High School in Littleton, Colorado, demonstrated that, left unchecked, hatred can led to an apocalypse. While most schools have plans in place to deal with fire, bad weather and medical emergencies, few are prepared for bias incidents. Here is an excerpt from *Responding to Hate at School,* published by Teaching Tolerance:

• Create an unwelcome environment for hate speech and symbols. Left unchecked, epithets, physical intimidation and hate graffiti create a toxic environment. Take a stand against hate literature, music, Web sites and E-mail. Designate one staff member to monitor hate Web sites.

• Speak up when bigotry comes from colleagues. We all harbor stereotypes, but, left unchallenged, teachers can easily transmit theirs to students and be insensitive to bias in schools.

• If a hate emergency occurs, focus on safety first. Take rumors of violence and bias incidents seriously. Set up a police liaison ahead of time. Set up a tip line or E-mail box for hate events and rumors.

• Support victims of harassment. Surround them with an atmosphere of protection and, if they wish, help from fellow students. Identify teachers or counselors as "safe contacts" for every type of bias event. Declare schools "hate-free zones."

IVORY TOWERS

As small communities in themselves, college campuses should adopt the recommendations in this guide for their use. Racial tensions should be aired, victims supported and hate crimes denounced by administrators. By practicing and teaching diversity, colleges influence attitudes and behavior in the leaders of the future.

One possible approach is the program adopted by Knox College in Galesburg, Illinois. The President's Council of Intercultural Concerns created a "Not on Our Campus" project which surveyed campus racial attitudes, encouraged reporting of bigotry, and organized both a bigotry response team and a long-range program of diversity, awareness and sensitivity workshops.

FOUR STEPS FOR PARENTS

1 Ask your schools whether curriculums and textbooks are equitable and multicultural.

2 Encourage teachers and administrators to adopt diversity training and tolerance curricula, *Teaching Tolerance* magazine and other diversity education materials.

3 Encourage your children to become tolerance activists. They can form harmony clubs, build multicultural peace gardens, sponsor "walk in my shoes" activities and join study circles to interact with children of other cultures.

4 Watch where your children are surfing on the Internet. Discuss the problem of hate sites openly, as you would the dangers of sex and drugs.

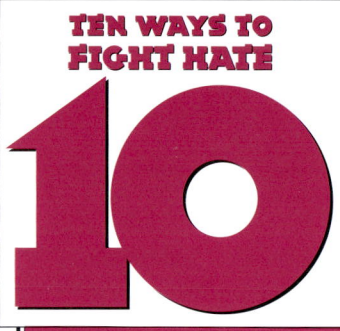

TEN WAYS TO FIGHT HATE
10
DIG DEEPER

LOOK INTO ISSUES THAT DIVIDE US: ECONOMIC INEQUALITY, IMMIGRATION, HOMOSEXUALITY. WORK AGAINST DISCRIMINATION IN HOUSING, EMPLOYMENT, EDUCATION. LOOK INSIDE YOURSELF FOR PREJUDICES AND STEREOTYPES.

SOONER OR LATER, ANY TOLERANCE EFFORT BUMPS UP against issues that will take more than a neighborhood to solve. Peeling away the face of hate reveals a country with deep, systemic and unresolved prejudice, discrimination and intergroup tension. These issues cry out for answers and people to take them on. As former white supremacist Floyd Cochran put it: "It is not enough to hold hands and sing Kumbaya." One of the leading civil rights clearinghouses, the Leadership Conference Education Fund in Washington, warns that failure to tackle the root causes of intolerance will leave the heroic efforts described in this guide looking "like small points of light in a sea of overwhelming darkness."

In any city and state there are dozens of problems to address: hunger, affordable housing, elderly isolation, domestic violence, school dropouts, etc. A caring group of people, having coalesced to deal with hate, could remain together to tackle any number of community chores and societal problems.

A NATION OF IMMIGRANTS: Michael Adeyoju of Ann Arbor, Michigan, is sworn in as a U.S. citizen 13 years after immigrating from Nigeria.

SIX ISSUES TO THINK ABOUT

A NATION OF MINORITIES

As the 21th Century began, New York City's million-student school system reported enrollment that was 38 percent black, 35 percent Hispanic, 19 percent white and 7.9 percent Asian/Pacific Islanders. In some California schools, 20 languages are needed in some classrooms to help kids learn English. Even in Hall County, Nebraska — home of farms, a meat-packing plant and fewer than 50,000 people — 30 different languages are being spoken in homes.

If recent trends continue, whites will lose their voting majority in several states between 2025 and 2050. By 2050, according to the President's Initiative on Race, "Asians, Hispanics, non-Hispanic blacks and American Indians together will approach 50 percent of the population." By the middle of the 21st Century, we will be, in effect, a country of minorities.

HAVE AND HAVE-NOTS

We are a country whose citizens are more united than divided – so concludes the President's Initiative on Race. But the cold statistics of the census remind us that the American dream is not equally shared. By virtually every indicator of success, people of color are at the bottom. More than 20 percent of African Americans and Hispanics live in poverty, compared to fewer than 10 percent of whites. For blacks, unemployment is about twice as high as for whites. Infant mortality for black babies is more than double that of whites. Despite gains by the civil rights and women's movements, minorities consistently report discrimination in "most domains of life."

THE FIGHT FOR WHITE SOULS ...

Hate groups recruit white males, women and children who have failed to realize their American dream. Oklahoma City demonstrated that men thought to be patriotic can be sucked into conspiracy theories and murder. The fear, outrage and powerlessness felt by people being tossed about by world economics are real. The answer is not to label them as "kooks" or isolate them and their fears. Potential recruits, whether laid-off auto workers, young skinheads, "Trenchcoat Mafia" members or Midwestern farmers, need to hear progressive voices and be recruited into community-wide and national efforts. They need to feel connected to society and to find outlets for their frustration with weapons other than guns and violence.

... AND BLACK SOULS

After holding blacks in slavery for 200 years, after officially discriminating and degrading them for another century and having still failed to ensure that America lives up to its promise, no one should be shocked that the black community has produced demagogues with large followings. They portray white America as evil and reject integration as illusory and dangerous. Whatever its source, hatred must be denounced as we encourage the disenfranchised to reject separatism and join in the struggle to create a just and multiracial society.

GAY RIGHTS

Some people oppose protection of gays and lesbians in civil rights legislation and refuse to join tolerance coalitions if gays are included. Like other victims of hate crimes, gays and lesbians are the target of jokes, harassment and physical harm because of who they are. Demonizing them, as a handful of vocal, conservative church leaders do, creates a field of bias in which more harmful attacks are inevitable. We believe that to focus on the sex act, as gay-bashers do, diverts attention from where it properly belongs — respect, and the sanctity of privacy and personal security that must surround every human being. The debate over "special" protection must not influence the fundamental requirement that every member of our society be guaranteed the right to "life, liberty and the pursuit of happiness."

HATE CRIME LAWS

Hotly contested and flawed by reporting inaccuracies, hate crime laws serve an important purpose. They alert us to tension and hatred between groups of people. A hate crime against an individual is also an attack on a class of citizens, a "message crime" intended to terrorize everyone in the class. Hate crimes threaten a community's health. They can trigger civil unrest and raise tensions between groups or between victims and authorities. Because of the great danger they pose, hate crimes warrant aggravated penalties. Hate victims are not asking for special rights, only for the freedom to live daily lives without fear.

WOMEN AS HATE VICTIMS

At least one women is raped every six minutes in America. Many others suffer intimidation, injury and death at the hands of men. Under federal law, the brutalizing of women is not considered a hate crime. A growing number of human rights organizations believe gender should be included in bias crime laws. There is no question that stereotypes, slurs, jokes and ongoing discrimination create an atmosphere in which women are made objects and targets.

WHAT ABOUT ME?

TOLERANCE, fundamentally, is a personal decision. It comes from an attitude that is learnable and embraceable, a belief that every other person on earth is a treasure. We each have the power to change our attitude to overcome our ignorance and fears, and to influence our children, our peers and our community. It begins with "me."

We all grow up with prejudices. It takes effort to see them as clearly as others do. Human rights experts recommend starting with our speech and thought patterns. Am I quick to label "rednecks" or "liberals"? Do I tell gay jokes? Am I careless with gender descriptions?

Ann Van Dyke, who leads tolerance workshops for the Pennsylvania Human Relations Commission, begins with her own story: "Nice Christian girl from a farm community, and not a clue I was full of bigotry until I moved to the big city. I was loaded with negative assumptions."

The Rev. Julian Walthall of Mobile, Alabama, recalls being told as a child that he was "better than 'they' were." As an adult, he works to overcome this, in part, by inviting people of color into his home for dinner and dialogue.

Here are some more questions you might ask yourself:

How wide is my circle of friends? How diverse is my holiday card list? How integrated is my neighborhood? Why is that? Do I belong to private clubs that exclude? Do I take economic segregation and environmental racism for granted? How often am I in the minority? Do I have the courage to tell a friend not to tell a sexist joke in my presence? How can I go out of my way to know people who appear different?

There are many good books, films and workshops to guide you in self-examination. Reading histories of the civil rights movement and other cultures is a good start.

THE IMPORTANT STEP IS TO BEGIN ...

"IT'S JUST ONE CRAZY, HAPPY FAMILY," says New Orleans Saints football fan Cat Fleuriet, right, of her sports friendship with Freda Williams, left. The two met at a Saints game.

RESOURCES
A COMPILATION OF ORGANIZATIONS AND MATERIALS THAT CAN ASSIST YOU IN FIGHTING HATE IN YOUR COMMUNITY

NATIONAL ORGANIZATIONS

Southern Poverty Law Center
Intelligence Project
Teaching Tolerance
400 Washington Ave.
Montgomery, AL 36104
(334) 956-8200
www.splcenter.org
www.teachingtolerance.org
www.tolerance.org

Anti-Defamation League
823 United Nations Plaza
New York, NY 10017
(212) 490-2525
www.adl.org

American-Arab
Anti-Discrimination Committee
4201 Connecticut Ave. NW, #300
Washington, DC 20008
(202) 244-2990
www.adc.org

American Jewish Committee
165 East 56th St.
New York, NY 10022
(212) 751-4000
www.ajc.org

Asian American Legal Defense
& Education Fund
99 Hudson St., 12th Floor
New York, NY 10013
(212) 966-5932

Center For Democratic Renewal
P.O. Box 50469
Atlanta, GA 30302
(404) 221-0025
E-mail: cdr@igc.apc.org

Community Relations Service
Department of Justice
600 E. Street N.W., Suite 6000
Washington, D.C. 20530
(202) 305-2935
www.usdoj.gov/crs

National Association for the
Advancement of Colored People
4805 Mt. Hope Drive
Baltimore, MD 21215
(410) 358-8900
www.naacp.org

National Conference for
Community & Justice
475 Park Ave. S., 19th Floor
New York, NY 10016
(212) 545-1300
www.nccj.org

National Council of Churches
475 Riverside Drive, Room 670
New York, NY 10115
(212) 870-2376
www.nccusa.org

National Gay & Lesbian Task Force
1700 Kalorama Road NW, Suite 101
Washington, DC 20009
(202) 332-6483
www.ngltf.org

Parents and Friends of
Lesbians and Gays
1101 14th St. NW, Suite 1030
Washington, DC 20005
(202) 638-4200
www.pflag.org

Simon Wiesenthal Center
9760 West Pico Blvd.
Los Angeles, CA 90035
(310) 553-9036
www.wiesenthal.com

Stop the Hate Initiative
Campus Hate Crime Prevention
Association of College Unions
International
One City Centre, Suite 200
120 W. Seventh St.
Bloomington, IN 47404-3925
(812) 855-8550
www.stophate.org

COMMUNITY-BASED PROGRAMS

Coloradans United Against Hatred
c/o American Jewish Committee
P.O. Box 11191
Denver, CO 80301
(303) 320-1742
www.cuah.org

Community Cousins
140 Encinitas Blvd., Suite 220
Encinitas, CA 92024
(760) 944-2899
www.cuzz.org

Facing History and Ourselves
16 Hurd Road
Brookline, MA 02445
(617) 232-1595
www.facing.org

Green Circle Program
c/o Nationalities Service Center
1300 Spruce St.
Philadelphia, PA 19107
(215) 893-8400

Not In Our Town
The Working Group
P.O. Box 10326
Oakland, CA 94610
(510) 268-9675
www.pbs.org/niot

Study Circles Resource Center
P.O. Box 203
Pomfret, CT 06258
(860) 928-2616
www.studycircles.org

REGIONAL ORGANIZATIONS

California Association of Human Relations Organizations
1426 Fillmore St., Suite 216
San Francisco, CA 94115
(415) 775-2342
www.cahro.org

Center for New Community
P.O. Box 346066
Chicago, IL 60634
(708) 848-0319
www.newcomm.org

Communities Against Hate
Youths for Justice
P.O. Box 10837
Eugene, OR 97440
(541) 485-0257

Montana Human Rights Network
Box 1222
Helena, MT 59624
(406) 442-5506
www.mhrn.org

Northwest Coalition For Human Dignity
P.O. Box 21428
Seattle, WA 98111
(206) 762-5627
www.nwchd.org

Pennsylvania Network of Unity Coalitions
P.O. Box 8168
Pittsburgh, PA 15217
(412) 521-1548

ANTI-BIAS AND DIVERSITY WORKSHOPS

A World of Difference Institute
Anti-Defamation League
823 United Nations Plaza
New York, NY 10017
(212) 490-2525
www.adl.org

The National Coalition Building Institute
1120 Connecticut Ave. NW
Suite 450
Washington, D.C. 20036
(202) 785-9400
www.ncbi.org

PUBLICATIONS

One America in the 21st Century: Forging a New Future and *Pathways to One America in the 21st Century: Promising Practices For Racial Reconciliation* are both available from:
The President's Initiative on Race
Government Printing Office
Superintendent of Documents, SSOP
Washington, DC 20402-9328

Responding to Hate at School: A Guide for Teachers, Counselors and Administrators
Teaching Tolerance
Southern Poverty Law Center
400 Washington Ave.
Montgomery, AL 36104
(334) 956-8200
www.tolerance.org/rthas

Building One Nation: A Study of What Is Being Done Today in Schools, Neighborhoods and the Workplace
Leadership Conference
Education Fund
1629 K Street NW
Washington, DC 20012
www.civilrights.org

Hate Crime Statistics
Federal Bureau of Investigation
1000 Custer Hollow Road
Clarksburg, WV 26306
www.fbi.gov/ucr/hatecm.htm

Every Victim Counts: Reform Hate Crime Reporting
Tolerance.org
Southern Poverty Law Center
400 Washington Ave.
Montgomery, AL 36104
(334) 956-8200
www.tolerance.org/evc

PHOTOGRAPHY CREDITS

COVER
Woman holds broken rock in hands (Eric Swanson – Swanstock)

INSIDE FRONT COVER
Children look through a fence vandalized with a swastika in Kenosha, Wisconsin. (*Milwaukee Journal Sentinel*)

PAGE 4
Dale Sparks — *The Dominion Post*

PAGE 6
Diane Bock

PAGE 7
James Saban

PAGES 8-9
Holly McQueen — *Rockford Register Star*

PAGE 10
Gary Gardner — AP Photo

PAGES 12-13
David Phillip — AP Photo

PAGE 14
Rommel Pecson — Impact Visuals

PAGE 15
Fred Zwicky — *Journal Star*

PAGE 16
Jesse Tinsley — *The Spokesman Review*

PAGES 18-19
Andy Levin

PAGES 20-21
Kathy Anderson — *The Times-Picayune*

PAGE 22
Jim West — Impact Visuals

PAGE 25
Kathy Anderson — *The Times Picayune*

INSIDE BACK COVER
"Josh" plays with the shield of a State Patrol trooper during a Klan March in Gainesville, Georgia. (Todd Robertson – *Gainesville Times*)

BACK COVER
Kindergartners make friends easily at Lusher Elementary school, a racially and culturally mixed school in Uptown New Orleans. (Kathy Anderson – *The Times-Picayune*)